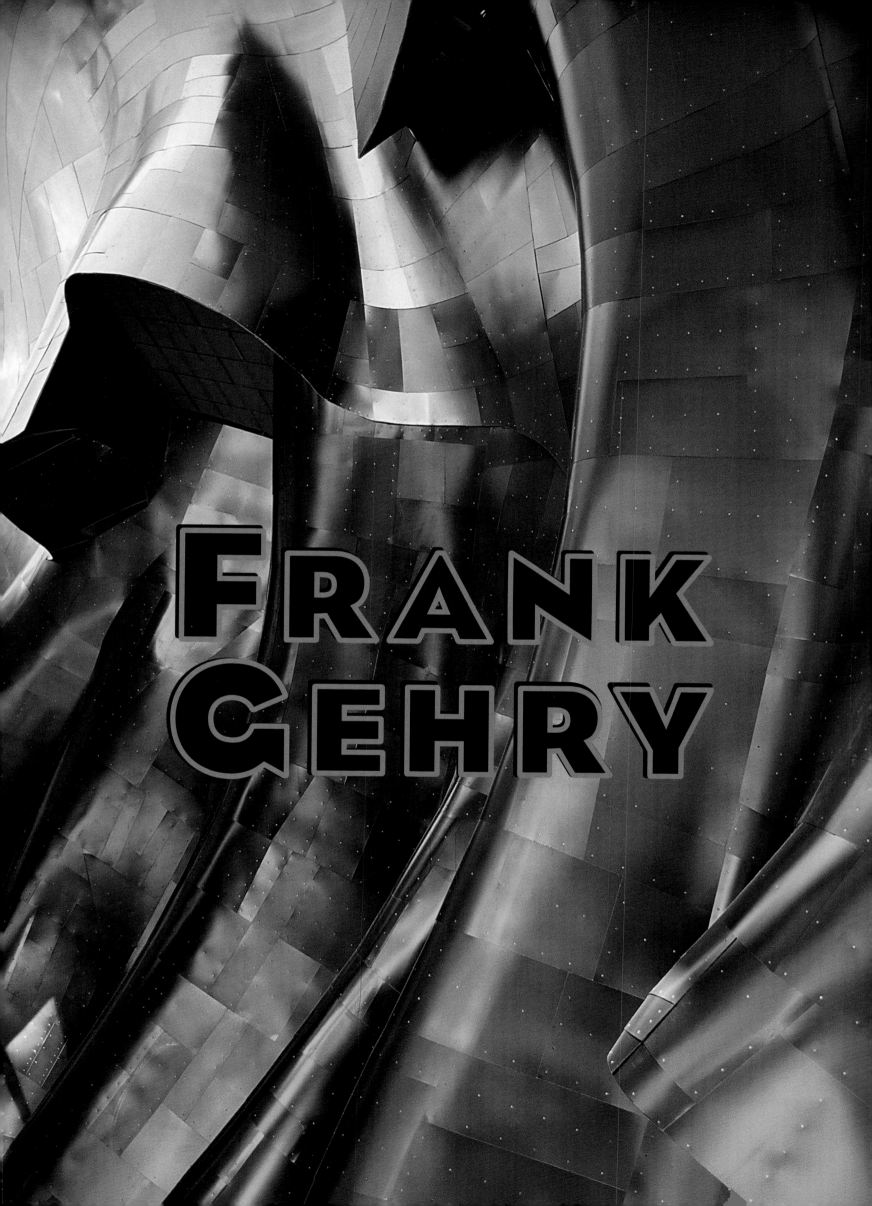

# FRANK GEHRY

# FRANK GEHRY

## JASON MILLER

BARNES
& NOBLE
BOOKS
NEW YORK

**A BARNES & NOBLE BOOK**

©2002 by Michael Friedman Publishing Group, Inc.

ISBN 0-7607-4630-3

Editor: Susan Lauzau
Art Director: Jeff Batzli
Designer: Midori Nakamura
Production Manager: Richela Morgan

Color separations by Chroma Graphics (Overseas) Pte. Ltd.
Printed and bound in Belgium by PROOST NV

1 3 5 7 9 10 8 6 4 2

# CONTENTS

# INTRODUCTION

# THE ARCHITECTURE OF CHAOS

*Life is chaotic, dangerous, and surprising. Buildings should reflect that.*
—Frank O. Gehry

The buildings of Frank Gehry, perhaps more than those of any other architect, effectively convey the tumult of life, but they embody as well life's energy, wonder, and abundant joy. His signature architecture employs sensuous curves, myriad volumes, and surprising materials and forms, challenging the viewer to figure out exactly how the building "works." But Gehry practices a regulated chaos, creating a realm in which buildings do unexpected things like swoop and sail but still function sensibly as habitable spaces.

The buildings also lead the viewer to wonder how the architect works. From what sort of mind do such designs spring, and how are these peculiar ideas rendered into structurally sound buildings? A look into the past, at some of Frank Gehry's formative experiences, and a glimpse of architecture's future, at the art and science of computer modeling, provide many of the answers.

Born Frank Owen Goldberg on February 28, 1929, in Toronto, Ontario, Gehry enjoyed a fairly typical middle-class childhood. He was an average student, with average interests. He played sports. He worked at his grandparents' hardware store. Like most children, he adored his grandmother, and thrived on the attention she gave him. The two would spend hours on the floor building "cities" out of scrap wood she collected from a neighboring shop. Frank also made playthings of common bushel baskets, bending and weaving the flat strips of wood into interesting shapes.

Every Thursday, Frank and his grandmother visited the market to buy a live carp for the family's Sabbath supper. They brought the fish home and placed it in the bathtub until it was time to make the gefilte fish. Young Frank watched the creature cruise the edges of the tub, a beautiful bit of enchantment finning slowly through the water. The next day the fish would be gone, but it remained suspended in Gehry's mind, an enduring symbol of nature's flawless blend of form and function.

Irwin Goldberg, Frank's father, had grown up in New York City, and retained a veneer of toughness, but Frank's mother, Thelma, took him and his sister on outings to museums and concerts, instilling in her children a lifelong love of art. When Gehry was about twelve, his father moved the family to a small mining town in Ontario, where Irwin opened a slot machine business. A shy kid, Frank continued to do well in school but, as the only Jewish boy in the small town, he also encountered anti-Semitism for the first time, and was constantly harassed by older, bigger boys. After the Canadian government banned slot machines, Irwin's business was ruined and the family went back to Toronto. Multiple business failures there took their toll on Irwin, and in 1947 Frank and his mother sold the family's possessions and organized a move to Los Angeles.

Far from living the American dream, the Goldbergs barely managed to scrape by in California. To support himself, Gehry went to work installing breakfast nooks, but enrolled in art classes at the University of Southern California to relieve the boredom of his job and to prepare himself for a better future. The family's losses and the uncertain new landscape left Gehry feeling underconfident and alienated, and he sought out L.A.'s vibrant art scene as a means of reconnecting with things he cared about. While still in school at USC, Gehry found his true passion: he visited an architectural site with a teacher and friend, and became entranced with the process, promptly switching his major to architecture.

During that time, he also met a young woman, Anita, who became his wife. Anita worked as a secretary so that Gehry could finish school, and in 1954 he graduated with honors. It was Anita who suggested that Frank change his name from Goldberg to Gehry, in response to the anti-Semitism he experienced both during his childhood in Canada and in school in the States. After Gehry served briefly in the army, the couple moved to Cambridge, Massachusetts, where Gehry planned to study urban development at Harvard. He hoped to effect real social change with innovative designs for affordable housing, but was soon frustrated by the university's staid approach to urban planning. Eventually, he had a falling out with one of his professors and returned to Los Angeles in 1957, disillusioned, to search for an approach to architecture more compatible with his politics. But Gehry's time at Harvard did yield one important outcome: he was introduced to the breadth of architectural history, including the buildings of Le Corbusier, whose reliance on the organic forms found in his own cubist paintings has been cited by Gehry as a powerful influence on his own architecture.

Over the next several years, Gehry worked for a number of different architectural firms, designing malls and a few residences, but was ultimately unsatisfied. He moved his family, which by this time included two small daughters, to Paris, where he worked for the firm of the renowned French architect André Remondet, and studied great works of architecture in his spare time.

When he returned to the States in 1962, he was ready to open his own firm, at first working with another architect but eventually operating simply as Frank O. Gehry and Associates. The small Santa Monica firm began soliciting commissions, with Gehry's first client offering him two thousand dollars to add a façade and a garden to a warehouse building. Clients slowly came, drawn to Gehry by word of mouth, and over the next decades he built a clientele that appreciated his interesting yet budget-conscious designs.

Stimulated by his pop artist friends and driven by his own restlessness, Gehry strove to include creative touches in his architecture, but often found himself constrained by the requirements of his commercial clients as well as by tight budgets. In some of his projects, Gehry began reinterpreting conventional designs with materials generally covered over or discarded, such as concrete block and plywood. Artist friends sometimes hired Gehry to design their homes and studios, and a noticeable dichotomy evolved in his work, with highly commercial projects paying the bills and experimental buildings feeding his imagination.

One day, as he worked, Gehry found himself staring at the edge of a piece of corrugated cardboard that was part of one of his project models. He began examining the material to see if it might have a practical application, and learned that when layers of cardboard were glued together they gained amazing strength. Gehry's college days, when he dreamed of creating affordable housing for the masses, came back to him, and he adapted this dream to encompass durable and economical furniture. From his original prototypes grew an entire line named Easy Edges. The

**Above:** The architect stands beside two of his signature creations, a cardboard chair from his Experimental Edges furniture line and a glowing fish lamp made from Colorcore. The lamp was the result of a design competition sponsored by the Formica Corporation for a new translucent plastic they called Colorcore. Frustrated by his first attempts to work with the material, Gehry threw his project to the floor and it splintered into dozens of pieces. The remnants reminded him of fish scales and he went to work renewed, ultimately producing this luminous lamp.

**Right:** Gehry's furniture is simply one example of his innate ability to look at materials and forms with a fresh eye. For this furniture line, cardboard—traditionally a throwaway packing material—is reinforced and reinterpreted to create pieces with permanence. Gehry ultimately discontinued his cardboard furniture collections, but persevered in his experiments with underutilized materials.

**Below:** Gehry poses in his bentwood workshop. Behind him are finished chairs and clamped molds for holding strips of maple.

chairs sold for only $35 and were so popular that Gehry, sensing that the project would engulf him and keep him from practicing architecture, ended production after only a few months. Five years later, he designed a similar, shaggier line of cardboard furniture, called Experimental Edges, but the line was not available commercially. He would again experiment with furniture in the 1990s, creating a line of elegant bent-maple chairs, tables, and ottomans that was inspired by the bushel basket musings of his childhood.

Gehry was excited by his foray into furniture design but still felt something lacking in his architecture, and he longed for more creative projects. Divorced from Anita, Gehry met and later married a young Panamanian woman named Berta Aguilera. It was the couple's own house—a small, pink, twenties-era bungalow in Santa Monica—that became Gehry's first landmark building. With the work on his house, Gehry stretched the term "remodel" to its very limits, changing not only the house's floor plan and vocabulary of materials, but also altering dramatically its footprint and essential character. The architect's growing fascination with industrial materials and sculptural forms led him to wrap the existing house in a sheath of corrugated metal punctuated by raw plywood, expanses of wire-embedded glass, and a half-shell of chain-link fencing that resembles a ballpark's backstop. What had been exterior walls now became interior ones, and internal workings such as plumbing, wiring, and wooden studs and joists were purposefully exposed.

Gradually, the house achieved a sort of local fame, as Gehry's artist friends and acquaintances visited and spread the word, and he was awarded new commissions based on his daring design. Taking as his inspiration modern art and the wealth of underutilized materials he saw around him, rather than the great buildings of earlier architectural history, Gehry sought to further blur the line between architecture and sculpture with each new building.

Eventually, Gehry decided to give up designing the more mundane malls and corporate offices that had been the mainstay of his firm in order to concentrate on architecture that energized him. In a scene that Gehry recalls somewhat gleefully, the president of the Rouse Company, one of Gehry's biggest clients, came to dinner at the renovated Gehry Residence and was struck by what he saw. He realized that Gehry could not possibly be equally enthusiastic about the wildly innovative remodel and his prosaic shopping mall designs, and advised the architect to give up his more conventional projects. Gehry took this advice, and began to rebuild his firm, focusing this time on commissions that would allow him to expand his range of materials and develop forms in imaginative ways.

One of his first such projects was the Loyola University Law School, near downtown Los Angeles, begun in 1978. Gehry listened to his clients, who wanted to foster a community atmosphere at the commuter school and also include visual references to the law. Facing budgetary restrictions, the school needed a flexible plan that would allow them to add to the campus as funds became available. Gehry had recently visited Rome, and fashioned a design that alluded to ancient ruins centered on a plaza, but also made use of his own idea of a "village of forms." While the buildings are arranged to appear as a cohesive whole, they feature diverse shapes, heights, and materials, including brick, concrete, sheet metal, Finnish plywood, glass, and yellow stucco.

Over the next decade, Gehry refined his concept of a village of forms and pushed the experiment further, introducing into his designs unorthodox forms like the Chiat/Day Building's four-story binoculars, which sit between a boat-shaped building and one that is abstractly treelike. As he found his architectural voice, Gehry increasingly introduced eccentric collections of sculptural forms rather than adhering to formal architectural principles.

Perhaps one of the architect's most instructive experiences was with a house that was never built, the Peter Lewis Residence. The decade-long story of this remodeling project began in 1987, when Gehry visited the site, agreed to a budget of approximately $2 million, and began creating studies. As his client added more and more stipulations, the project grew in scope until remodeling was no longer feasible; the existing house would have to be torn down. Gehry started again, working up a new design that included a huge fish pavilion overlooking the neighboring golf course. Assured of a battle with the community if he tried to make Gehry's design a reality, the client killed the project.

Later, the client again contacted Gehry and asked that his son work with Gehry to continue the design process. The son set forth a new series of demands and changes, including a $5 million sound system, a $5 million security system, a getaway tunnel, a panic room, and a 2,000-square-foot art gallery—unsurprisingly, the estimated cost skyrocketed as the project's parameters ballooned. The client again stopped the project. Over a period of nine years, the project was on again and off again, morphing each time with the client's changing demands, and was ultimately abandoned.

Despite its frustations, the Lewis Residence turned out to be a pivotal project for Gehry, serving as a laboratory for his evolving ideas about his village of forms concept. He was able to experiment freely with changing designs over a lengthy period of time, adding, deleting, and editing based on the client's wishes and on ideas contributed by the high-profile artists Lewis brought in to consult. But the process was ultimately worth Gehry's time and trouble: forms he toyed with and solutions he discovered while working on plans for the Lewis house would be reprised to stunning effect in later designs.

In 1989, Gehry was awarded the prestigious Pritzker Prize, commonly hailed as architecture's equivalent to the Nobel Prize. While the prize is typically reserved for an architect whose body of work is largely complete, the award jury chose to anticipate Gehry's lifetime achievement, recognizing his revolutionary designs when he was only at the midpoint of his career.

If the Pritkzer jury's motive was to spur Gehry to even greater heights, it accomplished its goal with the 1997 opening of the Guggenheim Museum in Bilbao, Spain. Gehry's most famous building to date, the Guggenheim Bilbao is fondly known to city residents as "the artichoke," perhaps as fitting a description as any. The museum encompasses 297,000 square feet (27,621m²) and is clad in gleaming titanium panels that change color with the shifting light. Sensuous forms curve and rise in a multitude of directions, resulting in a building that functions like a colossal piece of sculpture that must be viewed from every angle to be fully appreciated.

The Guggenheim Bilbao has achieved a level of fame rare for a piece of architecture: it has graced magazine covers and the front pages of newspapers; it appears in car commercials and music videos; and it continues to be a topic of interest in the architecture community, where it is applauded for its sweeping façade, fundamental eccentricity, and undeniable presence. And the building succeeds on a more practical plane as well. The Basque Country Administration had conceived of the museum as a way to both draw tourists to Bilbao and to celebrate the city's seven hundredth birthday; optimistic projections of 500,000 visitors a year have been surpassed by the nearly one million people that the museum draws annually.

The realization of Gehry's Guggenheim Bilbao design was a triumph not only of imagination but of technology, for without the help of an ingenious computer software program, the structure might never have been built. Gehry's methods had always been somewhat unorthodox for an architect. Instead of working with a T-square at a drafting board, Gehry habitually made frenetic sketches and then built model after model, using everything from paper and corrugated cardboard to wood and red velvet. The resulting designs were often challenging to build, and contractors were wary of the cost overruns that could occur if complicated building specs were miscalculated, not to mention nervous about estimating the amount of time the designs would take to execute.

A computer program rescued Gehry's less buildable designs from oblivion. Called CATIA (Computer Assisted Three-dimensional Interactive Application), the software had been developed in the late 1980s by French aeronautical engineers for use in building fighter jets. Gehry's staff proved invaluable in researching and applying the CATIA program, as the architect himself firmly refuses to learn the software, preferring instead to work with physical models as he has always done. Once Gehry is pleased with his scale model, the model is scanned into the computer using an electronic pen. The program then interprets the scan as a three-dimensional computer image, mapping each surface in detail. From the computer model, a final physical model and accurate architectural drawings can be created. The program also itemizes elaborate building specifications, allowing suppliers to produce titanium panels or stone blocks—or any other material of choice—to the exacting requirements of the design.

**Opposite:** This set of models represents part of the design process for the Disney Concert Hall in Los Angeles, California, which has a long and challenging construction history. After Gehry has made his sketches and an initial model, a member of his staff scans the physical model into the computer using the CATIA program. The software translates the information into a computer model (top photograph). Shading is added to the computer model, and the building is carefully reviewed (middle photograph). An accurate scale model (bottom photograph) is then built using the specifications created with CATIA, and is reviewed once more. When the design is finalized, the software can be used to test building structures, generate precise drawings for building plans, and produce lists of exact specifications.

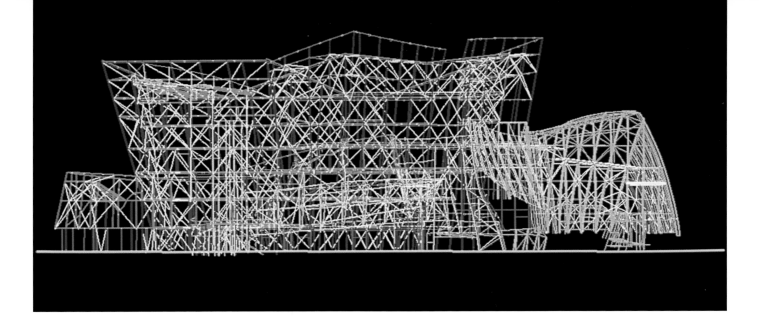

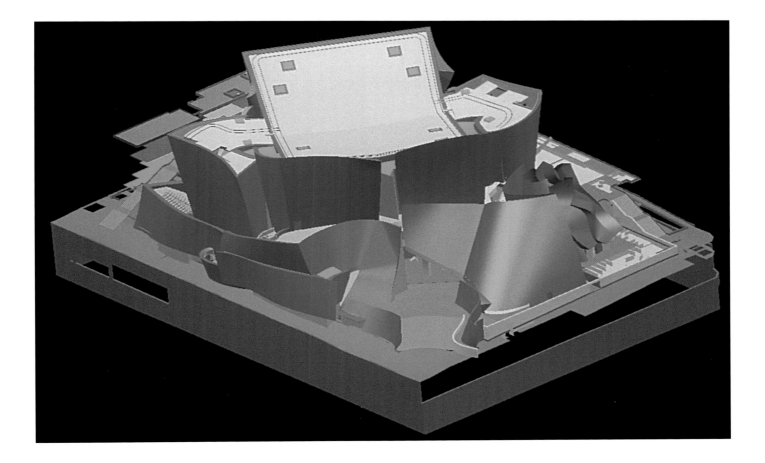

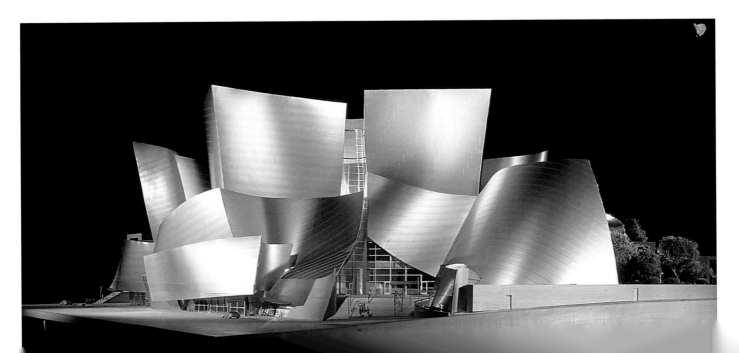

**Right:** Part of a growing body of piscine sculptures, Gehry's *Standing Glass Fish*, which belongs to the Walker Art Center and is permanently installed in the Cowles Conservatory, measures twenty-two feet (6.7m) in length and rises fourteen feet (4.2m) into the air. Suspended over a small rectangular pool, the fish is framed in wood and steel; its scales are tempered glass shards that have been assembled piece by piece using clear silicon as an adhesive.

**Left:** A sitting area in the Chiat/Day Building hosts a Gehry fish, continuing the aquatic motif prevalent throughout the architect's work. For Gehry, the fish represents perfection of form—sleek and elegant, its free movement is symbolic of creative energy.

**Opposite:** The Venice, California, offices of Frank O. Gehry and Associates hum with activity. Here, Gehry pauses in his studio amid the clutter of projects in various planning and modeling stages. The office interior was renovated in 1981 to expand the work space to 8,200 square feet (762.6m²).

A colossal fish sculpture planned for the Vila Olimpica in Barcelona was the first project for which Gehry and his staff used CATIA. The team had a minimum of time—less than a year—and a budget with little room for error, but the program lived up to its promise and the work was completed on budget and in time for Barcelona's 1992 Olympic Games.

CATIA has given life to Gehry's more fanciful projects, allowing him to transform the products of his imagination into physical reality. The buildings in the years that followed reflect this freedom, and are among his most famous: the Frederick R. Weisman Art Museum in Minneapolis, the Nationale-Nederlanden Building in Prague, the Guggenheim Museum in Bilbao, and the Experience Music Project in Seattle.

Despite the apparent diversity of Gehry's buildings, his work follows a discernable trajectory and draws upon certain powerful motifs again and again. A sculptor as much as an architect, he works intuitively, returning repeatedly to his favorite fish imagery. More-or-less literal representations of fish recur throughout many of Gehry's buildings in the guise of sculptures, lamps, skylights, and other elements, but piscine forms are also suggested in less tangible ways: in fluid curves, shimmering skins, and flashing movements. For Gehry, fish allusions are also a clever reply to postmodernism: where postmodernists mine architectural history for arcane classical references, Gehry looks beyond the historical past to prehistory for his own references.

Labeled a deconstructivist by many architectural critics for his abstract collections of apparently unrelated forms, Gehry himself resists the idea that he works within a strict category or with a particular established philosophy. However we might choose to define the architecture, the buildings themselves aren't meant to be simply viewed, but to be experienced. In his kinetic creations, Gehry continues to celebrate chaos, inviting us to rethink our concepts of what a building should be, to reexamine relationships between form and function as well as among forms, and, in his relentless use of throwaway materials, to reconsider the value of traditionally valueless things.

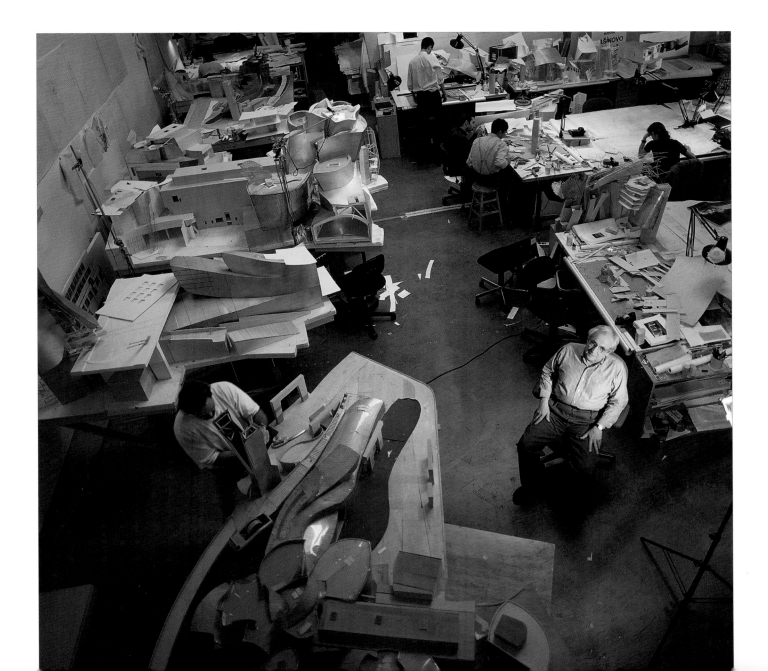

# Furniture Designs
## 1969-92
### Easy Edges Cardboard Furniture, 1969-73

**Left:** Frank Gehry's first furniture designs offered a daring yet inexpensive and versatile solution to the age-old problem of finding affordable furniture. Designed for commercial and residential applications, the Easy Edges line, which totaled seventeen pieces, was available in New York and Los Angeles at prices ranging from $15 to $115. The low price belied the strength and durability of the pieces: one popular image showed a Volkswagen Beetle perched atop four Easy Edges bar stools.

### Experimental Edges Cardboard Furniture, 1979-82

**Right:** In contrast to his Easy Edges designs, which were clean and linear, Gehry's Experimental Edges furniture was chunky, with greater overall mass and a more jagged silhouette. Using sections of commercial cardboard that had been employed chiefly in the manufacture of hollow-core doors, the architect fashioned a range of ingenious furnishings that were both comfortable and durable.

**Left:** Gehry began his Experimental Edges line without clear plans for commercial production, but between 1986 and 1988, New City Editions, a company he founded with two partners, marketed a dozen pieces. This model for an armchair reveals the layers of glued and laminated cardboard that make up the furniture.

**Left:** Gehry's bentwood furniture line, inspired by the bushel baskets he had played with as a child, was created for the Knoll Group. All of the architect's light and flexible bentwood furniture pieces were named after ice hockey terms—an homage to his favorite sport.

**Below:** A detail of the workshop shows the forms used to test various ways in which the wood strips can be bent.

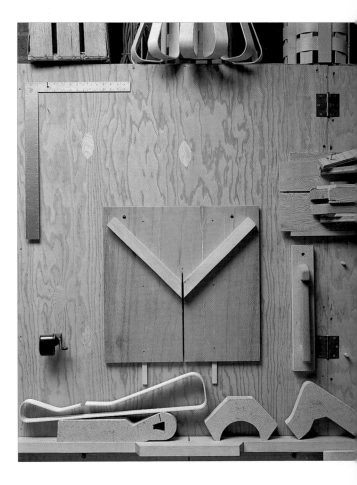

**Left:** The Gehry workshop, circa 1990, is cluttered with prototype chairs. In all, he created one hundred twenty different prototypes, which resulted in six chairs and a table being introduced in 1992. On the worktable to the right rests Power Play with Offside (the chair and ottoman, respectively).

# Danziger Studio and Residence

1964-65

Hollywood, California

**Below:** Completed in 1965, the Danziger Studio and Residence was one of Gehry's earliest forays into design with an urban context. The relatively small scale of the studio and residence, set into a busy neighborhood composed largely of commercial buildings, posed a challenge for Gehry: he had to make the structures part of the architectural landscape while creating a sense of privacy for the couple who would live and work there, a graphic artist and his wife. To help the buildings blend with the commercial flavor of the surrounding architecture, Gehry chose for the exterior a rough, raw stucco applied with a spray device, a mixture at that time reserved for the underbellies of freeway overpasses. The local building department balked, but Gehry persisted. He rented the necessary equipment, experimented on a friend's garage, then taught the technique to the plastering contractor.

# Merriweather Post Pavilion

## 1966-67
## Columbia, Maryland

**Below:** In the early 1960s, the Rouse Company developed an innovative urban plan for a new town called Columbia, to be situated midway between Baltimore and Washington, D.C. The concept called for a community with a deliberate layout and a carefully balanced mix of schools, businesses, shopping centers, recreational facilities, and homes, in studied contrast to the vast, uncontrolled urban and suburban sprawl that covered much of the American landscape. With its focus on urban planning, the Columbia project appealed to Gehry, and he ultimately designed four buildings for the town, including Merriweather Post Pavilion. For this open-air concert venue, Gehry was required to operate within the framework of the acoustical engineers' existing plans, which included two acoustical canopies. Set into a wooded park, the trapezoidal pavilion is not visible until approached from a network of footpaths; the site gave Gehry an opportunity to accent the sculptural possibilities of the building. The pavilion itself is composed of steel joists and a cantilevered roof, which is paneled in Douglas fir.

# Rouse Company Headquarters

## 1969-74
## Columbia, Maryland

**Right:** The Rouse Company Headquarters, another building in the planned community of Columbia, was designed for maximum flexibility. The company envisioned future additions, so both the north and south ends of the building were prepared to accommodate possible expansion. Interiors feature naturally lit walkways and a soaring atrium, along with a modular plan of acoustical and glass partitions that encompass open workstations as well as private offices and conference areas. Terraces topped with wood pergolas offer outdoor space for workers to relax, and lend the structure a profile resembling a ziggurat.

# Gehry Residence

## 1977-78; 1991-94
## Santa Monica, California

**The front façade** of Frank Gehry's home shows glimpses of the original 1920 pink bungalow wrapped inside the "architectural envelope" of corrugated sheet metal and chain-link fencing Gehry created in a 1977 remodel of the house. A later remodel of the remodel added a dense garden of succulents intended to make the house less accessible to intrusive architecture buffs, who have at times invaded the family's privacy. Gehry's unorthodox materials and eccentric approach to residential design infuriated his neighbors, many of whom signed petitions and pursued other legal means of halting his work.

**Below:** With views and access to the front yard, the dining room—like the rest of the Gehry residence—makes use of materials that are familiar but not usually found in a residential space. The exterior window, for example, is not only irregularly framed, it is glazed with the wire-embedded glass common in school settings. Originally one of the bungalow's exterior walls, the dining room's right wall is pink siding. Note, on the table, a model of Gehry's *Fish*, from Marina Village in Barcelona.

**Above:** Poised above the kitchen, a glass cube set at an angle creates an ingenious skylight. Visible, too, are the ceiling rafters and electrical wiring, which Gehry purposefully exposed when remodeling the 1920 house. (In later remodeling, the kitchen was made more spacious and the pastels were eliminated in favor of white.)

**Above:** The master bedroom, new to the 1990s remodel, is spare yet inviting, thanks to the warmth of wood on the walls and the exposed beams and roof timbers. Partially floored with glass and boasting a wide, built-in, glass-topped table, the master bedroom is also a source of light for the living room below, which benefits from the sunlight that filters down through these glass elements.

**Above:** A wall of windows with tilting support members creates an alcove in which Gehry's famous cardboard furnishings reside. As in other parts of the house, the architect has chosen unconventional materials, such as wire-embedded glass, raw lumber supports, and glass flooring.

**A massive cactus** anchors the rear terrace, which backs onto the kitchen. Floor-to-ceiling glass doors, which are fitted with retractable awnings, slide open to blur the distinction between indoors and out, while an upper deck carries out much the same function on the second story. Gleaming in the foreground is a lap pool sided with green Japanese tile.

**The campus** for the Loyola University Law School, which covers a full city block near downtown Los Angeles, is being completed in six phases, the first of which began in 1978. In response to the administration's desire that the campus make a statement about the law's historical traditions, Gehry borrowed classical elements that referred to the ancient Greek and Roman architecture of law. The Law School buildings, arranged around a plaza, create a "village of forms" intended to look as though it had grown up over many years, reinforcing the sense that the commuter school is a close and well-defined community. Completed in 1982, during the first phase of the school's construction, the vivid yellow Fritz B. Burns Student Center is divided in front by an airy greenhouse structure. A chunky, twisting staircase descends from the greenhouse to the courtyard below. In the foreground stands Claes Oldenburg's *Toppling Ladder with Spilling Paint*, installed in 1986.

**Below:** Merrifield Hall is modeled after a simple brick courthouse, reduced to its essential elements. Large-scale concrete columns across the building's façade are likewise stripped to their essence, and function more as sculpture than as architectural embellishment.

**Opposite:** Like other buildings on the campus, the North Instructional Building, a large lecture hall, references classical structures. In the spirit of postmodernism, Gehry combines age-old architectural forms with modern materials to create a building that acknowledges the past expressively yet unsentimentally.

**The column motif** is repeated in Donovan Hall, but for this building the columns have been extended to two stories, and are topped by lintels. To the right of Donovan Hall stands the chapel and its lighted campanile, a Gehry interpretation of a bell tower, in which no bell hangs. The chapel is framed in wood covered with copper sheet metal, and features wide expanses of glass.

# California Aerospace Museum and Theater

1982-84
Los Angeles, California

**An addition** to the original Aerospace Museum, which was housed in a 1913 brick armory, the new museum and its adjacent terraces, gardens, and 430-seat Imax theater was the only one of five planned new museum projects to be completed in time for the 1984 Summer Olympics. Composed of two separate forms, a polygonal tower and a basic stucco cube joined by an angled glass viewing wall, the new portion of the museum sits in front of the armory and is connected to it by a series of terraces.

**Above:** A forty-foot (12m)-high hangar door permits entry for the museum's typically oversized installations. In a tactic he claims was inspired by billboard advertisements, Gehry suspended a Lockheed F-104 Starfighter jet above the hangar door to visually announce the museum's contents.

**Above:** Inside the museum, a series of gangways and ramps lead to viewing platforms. Museumgoers enter on the mezzanine level, shown here, and are greeted by airplanes and satellites suspended from cables. Skylights flood the space with natural light. The interior's openness and Gehry's choice of construction materials pay homage to the aeronautics industry's birth in local hangars and warehouses.

# Norton Residence
## 1982-84
## Venice, California

**Above:** One of Gehry's favorite projects, the Norton Residence in Venice, California, aptly displays the architect's rare talent. The home, situated on a narrow beachfront lot, offers a cacophony of texture and color, plus privacy and ocean views for the owners. For this project, Gehry made use of an astonishing array of construction materials, including tile, stucco, concrete, and wood logs. Prominent in the west façade, shown here, is the freestanding study, designed to reflect the lifeguard stands that dot the beach. Also visible is the cube of glazed blue tile that forms the ground floor, as well as the second and third levels with their adjoining decks.

**Above:** A stairway leads from the main deck to the glass-backed study. Adjustable hurricane shutters take advantage of ocean breezes and prevent the diminutive space from becoming excessively hot.

**Left:** The kitchen, living, and dining areas reside on the second level. A two-story skylight that floods the kitchen with light continues up through the third-floor bedroom above.

# Rebecca's Restaurant

1982-85

Venice, California

**Below:** Later transformed into the Canal Club, which retained many of Gehry's design elements, Rebecca's Restaurant in Venice, California, offered a study in shock value. The 4,450-square-foot (413m²) space teemed with oversized aquatic sculpture made from a variety of materials. Here, a duo of alligators, constructed from crumpled aluminum, swims above a series of tables flanked by simple chairs and banquettes.

**Opposite:** Furnishings evoke an art deco sensibility, with overstuffed booth benches, glossy wood surfaces, polished stone tabletops, and a metal-edged bar. Exposed concrete, brick, stainless steel, glass and ceramic tile, and copper join to create a kaleidoscopic dining experience for restaurant patrons.

**Left:** An enormous beaded octopus floats upside down above the tables, reflected into infinity by a pair of mirrors on opposite walls. One of Gehry's signature fish sculptures leaps from the back of a booth, and, like the octopus, is endlessly multiplied.

**Winton Guest House**
1982-87
Wayzata, Minnesota

**Left:** The cluster of small buildings that compose the Winton Guest House was intended to offer playful contrast with the main house, designed in 1954 by modernist Philip Johnson, while remaining in sympathy with the main house's clean lines and simplified form. To be used primarily by the clients' extended family, the guest house incorporates various shapes, each containing an individual room.

**Above:** Living and dining spaces inhabit the tall, pyramidal structure roofed with a skylight. Joined to that is a boxy, reddish building clad in Finnish plywood that contains the kitchen and service functions; a galvanized metal sleeping loft tops the kitchen. Two other buildings—one a gently curved structure and the other a brick box (out of view in this photograph)—are bedrooms. A pair of glass-paneled doors provides entry into the elongated pyramid, a dramatic introduction to the house.

**Below and right:** Soaring ceilings, tall, high-set windows, and a skylight contribute a sense of light and air in the living room, and offer incomparable views of clouds and the surrounding trees.

**Below:** Nestled inside the curving wedge shape, a serene bedroom looks out on the landscape. Interior walls follow exterior lines, creating a space with flowing movement.

# Sirmai-Peterson Residence
1983-88
Thousand Oaks, California

**Above:** The 3,000-square-foot (279m²) Sirmai-Peterson house is set into gently rolling hills, and Gehry took great care to work with the grade of the site as he planned the house. Clad in galvanized metal, the main part of the residence suggests the form of a cross, with the living room, kitchen, and dining area housed in this segment. Across a small courtyard are two stucco bed and bath "blocks" connected to the public rooms via a bridge and an underground tunnel.

**Opposite:** In the dining room, a concrete block fireplace is literally the heart of the home, appearing in the center of the cross layout, where dining area, kitchen, and living spaces meet around a large concrete cube that contains storage space as well as the fireplace. The concrete block, exposed wood rafters, galvanized metal, and unpainted plywood are among the elements that lend the interiors Gehry's signature "unfinished" look.

**Spectacular reflections** of the Sirmai-Peterson
Residence are thrown onto the surface of the water basin,
which was created by damming an existing waterway.

# Chiat/Day Building
1985-91
Venice, California

-52-

**Below:** Three distinct façades comprise the Chiat/Day Building in Venice, California; the front of the building faces Main Street and its footprint extends to the property line on all sides. Making use of existing concrete warehouses, the renovation was designed to house the advertising agency's West Coast Corporate Headquarters, with space for staff work spaces, conference rooms, and storage.

**Opposite:** The most dramatic part of the building, the colossal binoculars, were designed in conjunction with artists Claes Oldenburg and Coosje van Bruggen. The driveway between the two segments of the binoculars gives access to the 300-car, underground parking structure; interiors of the binoculars provide meeting space.

**Opposite:** Reminiscent of a boat's prow, in acknowledgement of Chiat/Day's proximity to the ocean, this building relates visually to the beach-inspired commercial architecture along Main Street. The building's construction is designed to shade occupants from the summer sun; note the way that interior rooms are set back from the exterior shell, which is painted white to help deflect the sun's rays.

**Above:** Inside the curving structure, skylights stretch along the perimeter of the wall, flooding hallways and stairwells with natural light, which filters gently into the work spaces within.

**Above:** Glowing in a lighted niche that effectively recalls an aquarium, a signature Gehry fish sculpture draws viewers into the sitting area. As in many Gehry projects, aquatic imagery is found throughout the halls and rooms of the Chiat/Day Building.

**Below:** Many areas of the open-plan interiors are outfitted with lightwells, skylights, and reflective materials, like this copper sheeting, which encourages light to travel throughout the building.

**Above:** Above one of the "binocular" conference areas hangs a luminous lightbulb sculpture, a not-so-subtle reference to the creative impulses the room is designed to generate. Each of the cylindrical rooms is topped with a circular skylight.

## Schnabel Residence

1986–89

Brentwood, California

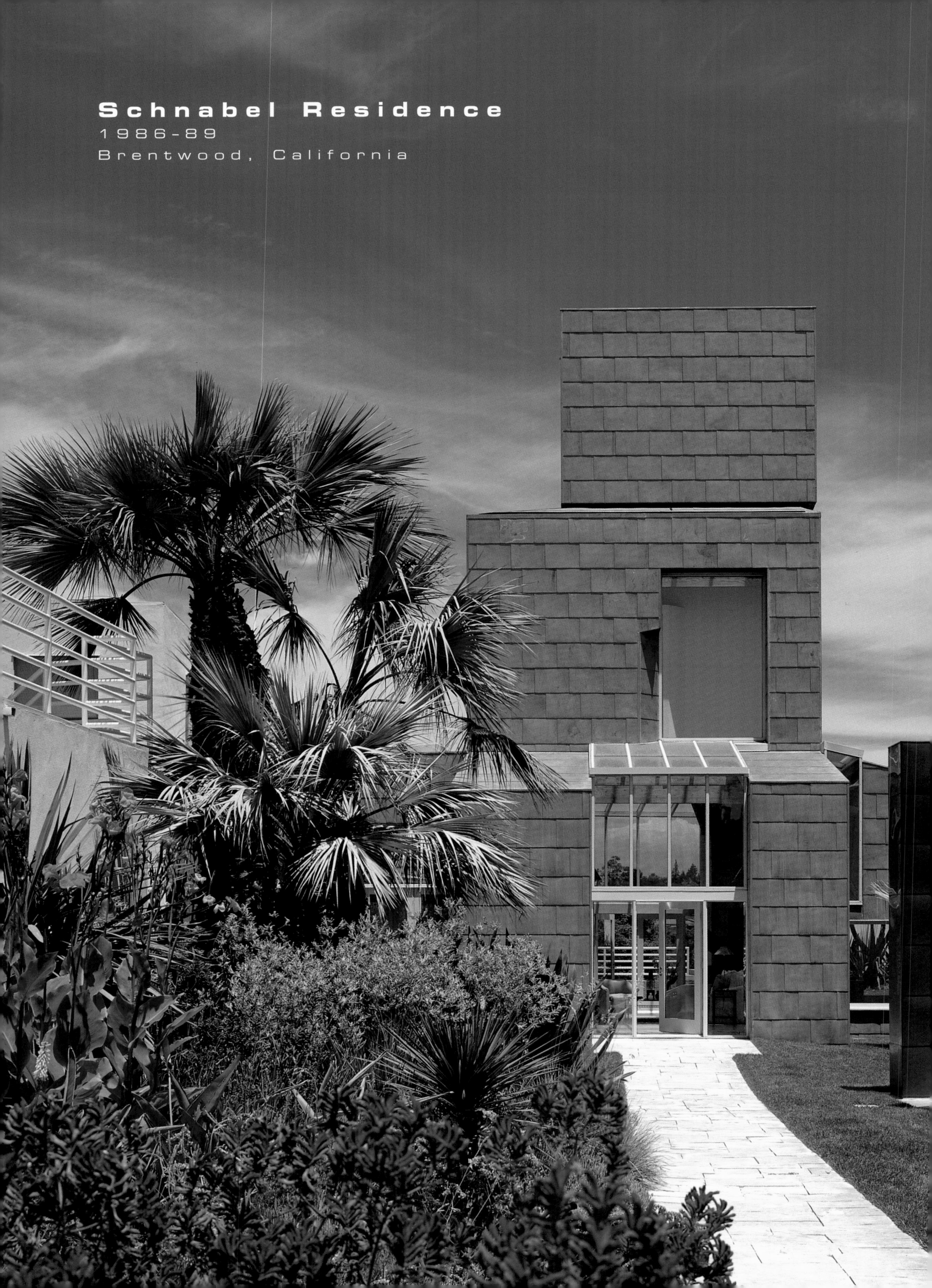

**Left:** The Schnabel Residence, like the Sirmai-Peterson Residence, is centered around a core of rooms in a cross formation; these rooms include the entryway, living and dining areas, and a library. This house repeats earlier Gehry themes—specifically a village character created with an arrangement of buildings of different forms and varying materials—though the Schnabel Residence is somehow more refined in its articulation of these differences. To the right of the main entrance is the guest house, to the left is the garage, above which staff quarters are located.

**Left:** This view reveals more distinctly the cruciform structure of the house's main segment, which is clad in lead-coated copper panels. A three-story tower topped by a skylight and punctuated by side windows on the second level floods the interior with light. Bordering the house to the south is a raised, tiled lap pool.

**Above:** The guest house stands slightly separate from the main part of the house, and away from the family room wing, the master bedroom pavilion, and a zig-zag-roofed studio/bedroom. On either side of the entrance stands a monumental copper-clad column, while a skylit roof is topped by a copper dome that recalls the Griffith Observatory—a place the client remembered fondly from childhood.

and a three-story skylight fill the sophisticated living room with light. Exposed beams and ceiling joists are familiar components in Gehry's work, but here these elements are used with restraint, achieving a subtler presence than they had in many of the architect's earlier projects.

**Opposite:** Adjoining the living room is the dining area, which also benefits from the sunlight that streams in through a network of skylights and windows. A built-in china cabinet holds dishes and glassware, and visually echoes the sets of double doors on opposite sides of the room. At the far end of the room is a short hallway that connects the main house's cruciform shape to a separate stucco structure containing the kitchen, a two-story family room, and two bedrooms.

**Above:** Sequestered on a level lower than the other elements of the house, the master bedroom is actually a pavilion set in a shallow, man-made lake; the suite is a private getaway that includes a bath, a sauna, an exercise room, and dressing rooms. As in many of the architect's buildings, extravagant glazing is a theme in the bedroom, where the pavilion skylight is a triumph of both art and practicality. Because direct rays falling right onto the bed would be contrary to the room's function, the sculptural skylight has a raised roof that helps shield the occupants.

**Below:** Viewed from the east, the house virtually glows as the sun sets and interior lights begin to be switched on. Without the visual distractions present in the daytime, it's easier to appreciate the myriad geometric forms that make up the structure.

**Right:** From the across the water-filled lower terrace, the master bedroom pavilion and its accompanying suite of rooms is visible, as are the main house, the kitchen/family room/bedroom wing to the right, and the studio/bedroom to the left. Farther in the distance, the dome of the guest house curves above the main house's silhouette.

**Sandwiched between** the Disneyland theme park and the Santa Ana Freeway, the Team Disneyland Administration Building presents two discrete façades. To passersby and staff members approaching from the east, a sunny yellow stucco face seems to billow and wave, articulating Disney's relationship to fantasy and playfulness. Cantilevered awnings made of galvanized metal shelter ground-floor windows and entries.

**Below:** Stainless steel panels cloak the west façade of the Administration Building, which stretches for almost 900 feet (274.5m) along the Santa Ana Freeway. The panels were washed with acid and blasted with tiny beads to achieve this opalescent, rainbow effect. Along the base of the façade, stretching its entire length, is a steel "rake."

**Left:** A closer view of the rake, from the side, reveals why Gehry calls it a cowcatcher, a reference to the wedge-shaped frames attached to the front of locomotives and designed to push obstacles off the track.

**Above and opposite:** The four-story entry atrium of the 330,000-square-foot (30,690m²) building was embellished with an enlarged painting of Goofy on bubblegum pink walls; the view, however, is of the cartoon dog from the inside. Sweeping curves and whimsical artwork capture the spirit of Disney without succumbing to saccharin sweetness. This atrium is the only interior space in the Team Disneyland Administration Building that was designed by Gehry.

# Center for the Visual Arts

1989
University of Toledo
Toledo, Ohio

**Above:** A glass wall encloses the courtyard formed by the L-shaped building. The three-story structure contains studios and classrooms on the upper two floors, where natural light is abundant. Spaces in which functions are less dependent on natural light, such as administrative offices, a library, and galleries, are housed on the ground floor and basement levels.

**Opposite:** Originally housed in the Toledo Museum of Art, the Center for the Visual Arts has been designed as a distinct entity that remains in sympathy with the neoclassical styling of the adjoining museum. The Center's cubist and sinuous sculptural forms carve a unique identity for the building, yet the green-tinted windows and the subtle iridescence of the lead-coated copper respond to the older museum's more august materials.

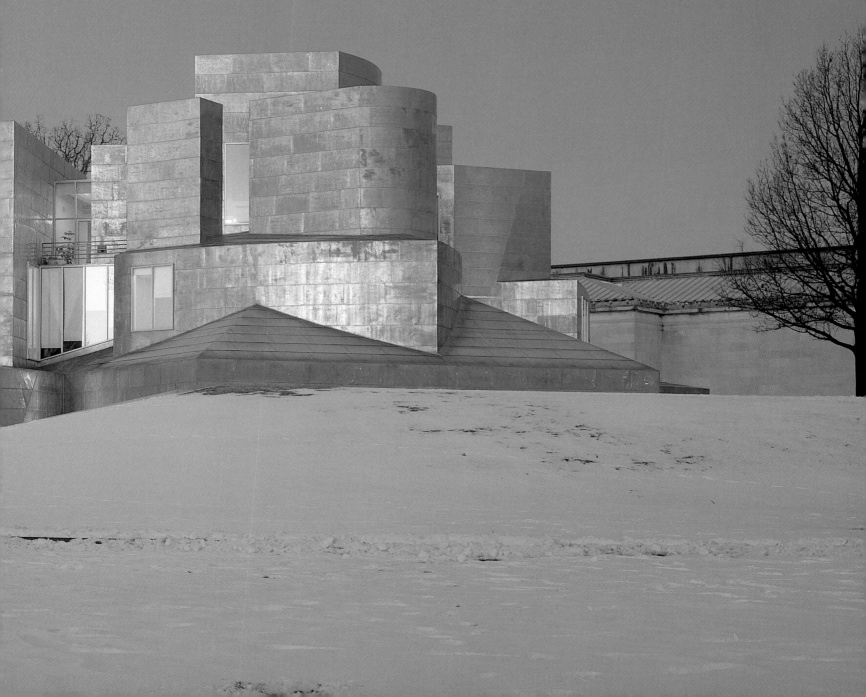

**The winter sun** reflects gently off the iridescent surface of the Center's lead-coated copper panels. This view from the north shows the site's thoughtful landscaping: a berm of earth rises toward the walls of the library, helping to shield this quiet space from outside noise.

# Walt Disney Concert Hall

## 1989-
## Los Angeles, California

**Beset by fund-raising difficulties,** the Walt Disney Concert Hall has expanded and contracted in design several times due to such considerations as acoustics, budget, and timing. While the complex will encompass gardens and terraces, gathering areas, offices, a café, and a gift shop, the building's focal point is undoubtedly the 2,400-seat concert hall—new home to the Los Angeles Philharmonic. To understand how to create a space that was exquisite both visually and acoustically, Gehry visited several concert halls in different parts of the world, then consulted with musicians and conductors and brought in expert acoustician Minoru Nagata. Gehry's interior hall design eliminated socially divisive balconies and used a series of smaller seating clusters to foster a close connection between the orchestra and its audience. Large-scale models were built to test the interplay between the orchestra platform, the ceiling, and the pipe organ. The final interior resembles a great ship, with the philharmonic on deck and the audience surrounding it on all sides.

# Frederick R. Weisman Art and Teaching Museum

1990-93
University of Minnesota
Minneapolis, Minnesota

**Below:** Set high on the eastern bank of the Mississippi River, the Frederick R. Weisman Art and Teaching Museum is Gehry's first all-new art museum (his previous museum designs were annexes to existing buildings or renovation projects). Part of the University of Minnesota campus, the museum incorporates several brick façades (visible to the right) that connect it to the other buildings on the university mall.

**Right:** University administrators claimed that they did not want "another brick lump," and Gehry satisfied this wish, creating beautifully sculptural volumes clad in stainless steel for the balance of the building. A seemingly random gathering of cubist forms, including sliced cones and cylinders, adorns the west façade, which is, in fact, a true façade: behind the stainless steel contortions lies a pragmatic, rectilinear building.

**Below:** Supported by sturdy legs reminiscent of tree trunks, a stainless steel canopy shelters the main entrance to the museum.

**Right:** Beyond the museum's brushed stainless steel panels are innovative yet highly functional gallery spaces. A lobby that wraps around three sides of the building offers access to the galleries on the interior side, as well as wide views of the river and surrounding landscape. The museum's main floor also includes a 120-seat auditorium with oversized sliding doors that open onto the lobby, blurring the separate identities of these spaces.

FREDERICK R. WEISMAN

**Guggenheim Museum Bilbao**
1991–97
Bilbao, Spain

**Among the most widely recognized** and critically praised buildings of the twentieth century, the Guggenheim Bilbao visually joins the Basque city to the surrounding landscape and delivers a significant piece of Bilbao's redevelopment puzzle. A partnership between the Basque Country Administration and the Simon R. Guggenheim Foundation, the Bilbao Guggenheim continues the bold architectural precedent set by Frank Lloyd Wright's design for the original Guggenheim Museum in New York City, yet resides comfortably on the industrial riverfront of the seven-hundred-year-old city. At the museum's entrance, a public plaza connects the building to the old city, and encourages meandering toward the neighboring Museo de Bellas Artes, the Old Town Hall, and the Universidad de Deusto.

- 88 -

- 89 -

**Left:** An aerial perspective shows the upper portions of the museum at sunset, with the atrium skylights just in view and the grandiose architectural forms unfolding like silvery petals.

**Below:** Viewed from the northwest, the museum's walkway extends over a portion of the Nervión River, and is punctuated at one end by a gargantuan sculpture of a spider named *Mamán*, by sculptor Louise Bourgeois.

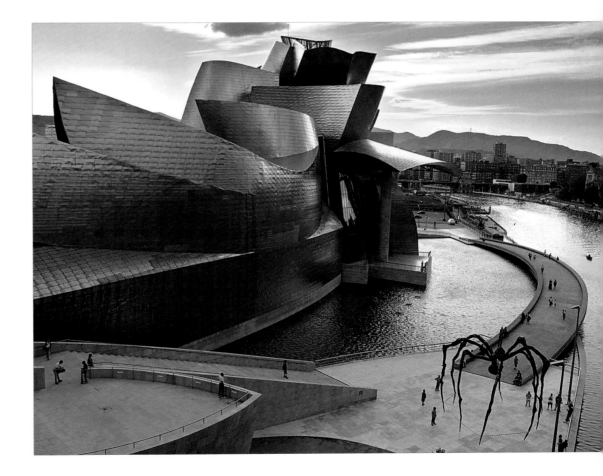

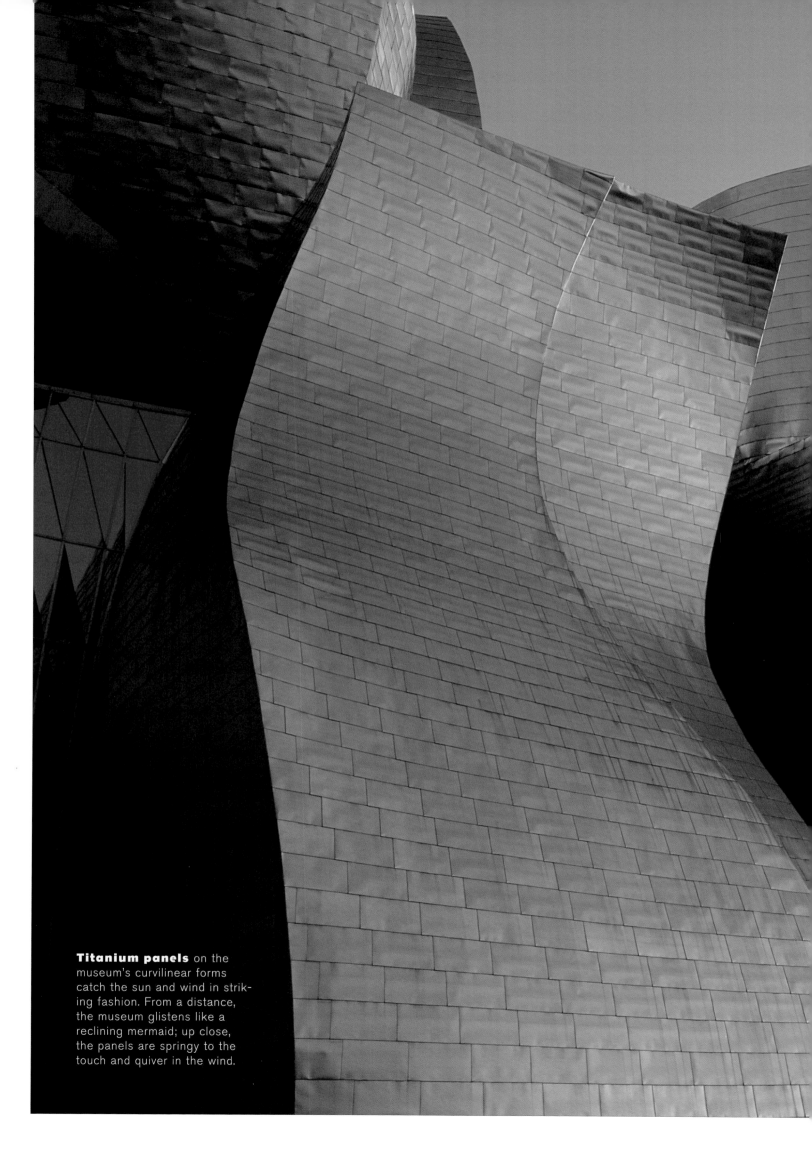

**Titanium panels** on the museum's curvilinear forms catch the sun and wind in striking fashion. From a distance, the museum glistens like a reclining mermaid; up close, the panels are springy to the touch and quiver in the wind.

**Opposite:** Skylights and immense glass walls that relate visually to the titanium panels allow daylight into the museum. The glazing was formulated to protect valuable works of art from heat and radiation, and special blackout shades on the skylights allow curators to regulate light as needed.

**Right, top:** Descending a flight of stairs, visitors pass the museum's regal nameplate on their way to the main entrance, which is framed with Spanish limestone and glass. Once inside the doors, they enter a spectacular atrium.

**Right, bottom:** Leaving the Guggenheim, museumgoers walk up toward the more traditional architecture of Bilbao. The museum's site, slightly below the level of the city, allows the monumental structure to become a charismatic part of the cityscape without completely overwhelming neighboring buildings with its presence.

**Above:** The central atrium, filled with an array of vertical forms and capped by myriad skylights, rises more than 160 feet (49m) into the air. Museum director Thomas Krens requested an entry space to rival that of the New York Guggenheim, and Gehry conceived this breathtaking atrium as an "idealistic city."

**Right:** A portion of the Boat Gallery, a tribute to Bilbao's heritage of shipbuilding and trade, showcases a steel sculpture by Richard Serra. The Bilbao Guggenheim was specifically designed to accommodate the large-scale works prevalent in twentieth-century art.

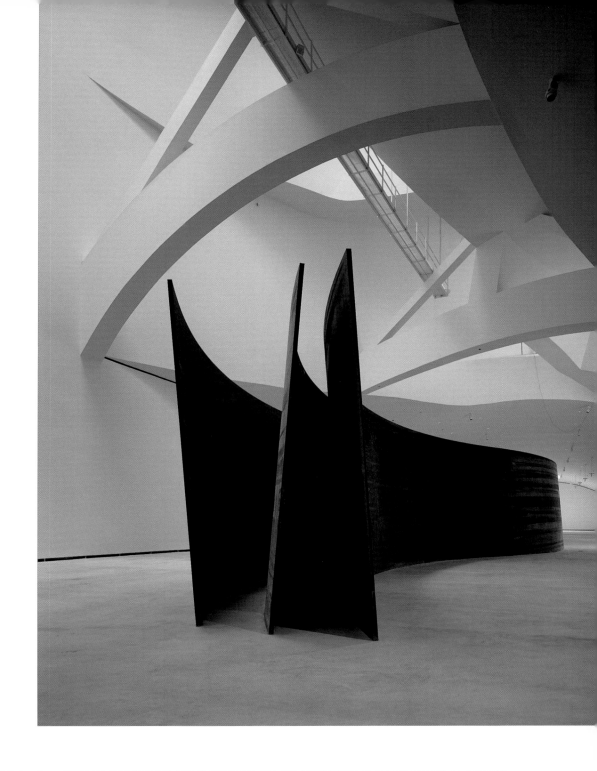

**Below:** Dramatic bridges, stair towers, and glass-encased elevators connect the various levels of galleries, which radiate outward from the atrium. This view from an upper level shows visitors moving along and beneath sinuous, whitewashed forms, drawn deeper into the museum by its awe-inspiring design.

**At night,** the museum casts its reflection onto the slow-moving waters of the Nervión River, which flows along the north side of the building.

# Nationale-Nederlanden Building
## 1992-96
### Prague, Czech Republic

**Below:** With inspiring views of the Vltava River and the city's skyline, the Nationale-Nederlanden Building dances joyously in Prague's historic district, an area where new construction is strictly regulated. Gehry's exuberant design was chosen in part because it acknowledged the corner site's role in anchoring a nearby public square and a well-traveled bridge.

**Opposite:** Known colloquially as Fred and Ginger, the towers that front the building are the epitome of functional grace. The curvaceous glass "Ginger" tower is made of arching vertical steel beams set with glass panels; the nipped waist of the building maximizes views from adjacent buildings and allows the skirt to billow convincingly. "Fred" is the more solid of the two, and the surface of this tower continues the undulating lines begun in the primary façade—both of these volumes feature staggered windows, rhythmic curving lines, and a restrained height that complements nearby historic townhouses.

# Albert H. Vontz Center
# for Molecular Studies

1993-99
University of Cincinnati
Cincinnati, Ohio

**Above:** Like several of Gehry's earlier residential works, the Albert H. Vontz Center for Molecular Studies exploits a cross-shaped layout, in which state-of-the-art laboratories run along the north-south axis, with offices along the shorter east-west axis. At the juncture of the cross' arms is a central atrium with common areas and elevators to other levels. The west side of the building displays its vertically and horizontally bulging walls and oversized, boxed-out windows with views to the multiple levels within.

**Above:** Inside the building, a central atrium features lounges and meeting areas, here furnished with Gehry's bent-maple chairs.

# Der Neue Zollhof
## 1994-99
### Düsseldorf, Germany

**Below:** Part of a harborfront revitalization project, the three buildings of Der Neue Zollhof (The New Customs House) are set along the Rhine River in downtown Düsseldorf: the center building is sheathed in polished stainless steel, its neighbor to the east is covered in white plaster, and the west tower is red brick. Separate structures, each with a myriad of volumes, allowed the complex its requisite square footage while permitting an open site plan and minimizing disruption of river views from existing buildings.

**Right:** Each tower was composed of "fingers," all centered around a main hub, providing discrete and flexible spaces for a number of different companies. Note that the windows of all three buildings can be opened to take advantage of cool breezes coming off the river.

**Left:** The center building, with exterior walls reminiscent of hanging fabric, is sited back from the waterfront, creating a plaza that tenants from all three buildings can enjoy. The buildings' configuration provides water views for a maximum number of offices.

# Pariser Platz 3
## 1995-2001
## Berlin, Germany

**Left:** Because of city planning constraints, the façades of the Pariser Platz 3, also known as the DG Bank Building, are uncharacteristically conservative; clad in limestone, they follow, albeit loosely, the lines and proportions set by other buildings in the vicinity. But inside the largely rectilinear structure lies a brilliantly fluid mixed-use space— the building encompasses both headquarters for the DG Bank and forty residential apartments.

**Above:** Perhaps the most inspired element in the Pariser Platz 3 is a four-story stretched–stainless steel sculptural form that resembles a prehistoric horse's head; within the skull is a wood-framed oval conference hall. High overhead looms a two hundred-foot (61m)-long fish-shaped skylight made of glass laid over a steel-wire frame. Beneath the atrium's floor—which is partially covered with a multifaceted dome of glass that functions as a skylight for the space below—are a lecture hall, the bank's cafeteria, and a spacious foyer.

**Above:** The interior of the oval conference room is paneled with thin strips of red oak that curve and weave through the space like muscle and sinew over bone, continuing the metaphor of the horse's head. Reportedly, the room was booked for a series of conferences based only on the promise of the model.

# Experience Music Project (EMP)

## 1995-2000
## Seattle, Washington

**Below:** Commissioned by Paul Allen, cofounder of Microsoft and ardent Jimi Hendrix fan, the Experience Music Project (EMP) celebrates the vitality and iconoclasm of American rock music with a building that is as creative and free-form as the music itself. The 140,000-square-foot (13,020m²) structure, which carried a $100 million price tag, is made up of six separate exhibit and public spaces that fit together like a three-dimensional puzzle. The forms and colors were inspired by the guitar, with multiple allusions to smashed guitars, a recurring performance motif of Hendrix's. As with other buildings, Gehry's staff used computer software to create a structurally sound representation of the architect's concepts and to engineer the complex building systems and elements. This view shows the EMP from the rear, as it appears from the Space Needle.

**Right:** The Seattle Center monorail runs right through the EMP, connecting the museum to downtown Seattle and giving passengers a brief glimpse of the building's interior. This literal motion penetrates the space, emphasizing the sense of movement integral to the majority of Gehry's works. Above the monorail's entrance are surging architectural forms that fulfill Paul Allen's directive that Gehry design a "swoopy" building.

**Left and above:** Sweeping glass plates supported by steel rods and I-beams hover over the building's central form, which is clad in painted aluminum. The ribbons of glass are meant to evoke guitar strings, while the red aluminum cladding was inspired by the old trucks rock 'n' roll legends once drove and, according to Gehry, will eventually fade like the finish of a vintage vehicle.

**Left:** The nearby Space Needle, built for the 1962 World's Fair and still Seattle's number-one tourist destination, casts its image on the highly reflective surface of EMP's polished stainless steel walls.

**Above:** Despite the building's overall mass, the front entrance of EMP presents a relatively low-slung silhouette along Fifth Avenue, in keeping with Gehry's wish not to dominate the neighborhood with an imposing façade. This street-level view of the entrance highlights some of the contrasts in material and palette that are evident throughout the building. For this project, the architect drew on a wide vocabulary of structural materials and finishes, including steel framing, cast-glass tile, titanium wire, stainless steel sheet metal, and autobody-paint-coated concrete. The Turntable Restaurant is visible through the goblet-shaped window.

**Above and opposite:** The EMP's "skin" is a story in itself. Uniquely sized and shaped stainless steel and painted-aluminum shingles—numbering upward of twenty-one thousand—were each individually cut, shaped, and installed seven to a panel. Completed panels were then fastened to the building's steel skeleton. EMP's exterior palette contains a number of musical references: blue for a Fender guitar, bead-blasted gold for a Les Paul, and of course, mirrored purple as a visual ode to Hendrix's "Purple Haze." The result is a rhythmic presence that introduces the musical history explored within the building.

**Above:** Looking down the stairs from the main lobby, the view is of the street level—where the group entrance, the Turntable Restaurant, and the museum store are located. Flowing walls follow the forms of the building's shell.

**Above:** At the bottom of the stairs, gazing up into the main lobby, museumgoers are greeted by a boatlike structure of polished stainless steel floating above the space. Note the exposed structural ceiling and support beams.

**Right:** The Demo Lab is a venue for performances, workshops, and educational programs, all held in the spirit of EMP's cultural mission, which is achieved with a highly interactive flair. The lineup is as eclectic as the museum itself, and includes music mixing and dancing. Presiding over the space, a fantastical mirror ball alludes to the days of disco.

**Left:** *Roots and Branches* is an almost magical work of art by acclaimed German-born artist Trimpin. Made up of more than five hundred guitars, plus drums, keyboards, and violins, the hands-on sculpture is complete with a computerized panel that lets visitors "play" the different instruments, offering both a visual and an auditory introduction to the museum's contents.

**Opposite:** Sky Church, EMP's grand hall, party space, and performance venue translates into reality the Jimi Hendrix vision of a place where people of all races, ages, and backgrounds can gather and listen to music. Near the top of the eighty-five-foot (26m)-high ceiling is a massive video frieze—the largest indoor video wall in the world. The room, which can hold up to a thousand people, boasts state-of-the-art lighting and acoustics.

# Condé Nast Cafeteria
## 1997-2000
## New York, New York

**Left:** The employee cafeteria at Condé Nast headquarters in New York City incorporates billowing, curtainlike sheets of glass—of which no two are alike—that define each eating area in the 260-seat cafeteria. Outside walls are lined with blue titanium panels that refer visually to the Bilbao Guggenheim, but these examples are perforated and backed with acoustical panels to prevent the space from becoming too noisy. Curving, high-backed banquettes in the main dining area border tables topped with ash plywood; adjacent to the dining area are a servery and four private dining rooms used for meetings. The opulent space invokes the power lunch culture prevalent at media giants, but levels the playing field by applying the trappings of upscale restaurants to the company's common area.

**Left:** Designed by Gehry's equally daring contemporary, Rem Koolhaas, the Guggenheim Museum in Las Vegas hosted a Gehry-designed exhibition, *Art of the Motorcycle*, after the show's unveiling at the Solomon R. Guggenheim Museum in New York. More than 120 motorcycles, set amid a weaving sea of metal, comprised the exhibition, which celebrated the design history of this beloved symbol of freedom and rebellion. The exhibit's enormous glazed box is made of glass panels laminated with an iridescent coating. From certain angles the surface of the box is opaque, and throngs with projected images of motorcycles in motion, but from other perspectives the glass is transparent, allowing the viewer to see the motorcycles encased inside.

**Above:** A ribbonlike metal "road" supports motorcycles that appear to be wending their way toward the rise in the background. As museumgoers walk through and among the curving metal sheets that partially frame the exhibit, they see themselves and the motorcycles reflected in the polished surface, as if in a funhouse mirror.

# INDEX

# PHOTO CREDITS